HEAVEN OR HELL

J.C. Melek

WESTBOW
PRESS®
A DIVISION OF THOMAS NELSON
& ZONDERVAN

WestBow Press books may be ordered through booksellers or by contacting:

WestBow Press
A Division of Thomas Nelson & Zondervan
1663 Liberty Drive
Bloomington, IN 47403
www.westbowpress.com
1 (866) 928-1240

Because of the dynamic nature of the Internet, any web addresses or
links contained in this book may have changed since publication and
may no longer be valid. The views expressed in this work are solely those
of the author and do not necessarily reflect the views of the publisher,
and the publisher hereby disclaims any responsibility for them.

Any people depicted in stock imagery provided by Thinkstock are models,
and such images are being used for illustrative purposes only.
Certain stock imagery © Thinkstock.

ISBN: 978-1-5127-6732-2 (sc)
ISBN: 978-1-5127-6733-9 (e)

Library of Congress Control Number: 2016920234

Print information available on the last page.

WestBow Press rev. date: 12/02/2016

I dedicate this book in memory of Sandra Sue Durham.

Along with her and her family, we hope there will not be one single person left on this earth who does not know what true *love* is and what it feels like to be truly *loved* by your true heavenly Father. We hope that not one person shall perish.

CONTENTS

CONTENTS

Acknowledgments

I would like to thank Vickie, Kim, and Tammy for all their help. I would not have been able to complete this book without it.

I also would like to thank Lance for his insight and his help in completing this book. It could not have been done without him.

But most of all I would like to thank my Lord and Savior Jesus Christ for helping and allowing me to write this book.

To Him be the glory

CHAPTER 1

IN THE
BEGINNING

On a cold, brisk Halloween night in 1954, kids were running up and down the street trick-or-treating. They were all dressed up in their favorite costumes, laughing and collecting as much candy as their bags would hold. They were so excited. I was excited too. It was for a different reason though. Trick-or-treating was not going to happen for this girl.

What was happening to me caused me so much pain and fear, a fear I had never experienced before. My palms were sweating, and I felt sick to my stomach. I was dizzy, and my heart was pounding. It felt as if it was going to jump out of my chest. The more the pain increased, the more my fear grew. I didn't know how to handle what was happening to me. I only knew this pain and fear had to stop. *Dear Lord, please make this pain and fear go away*, I prayed. It was so painful—an unbearable pain. I was so afraid, and I hurt more than I ever had in my entire life.

At the time, I was seventeen years old, married, and

pregnant. I felt all kinds of emotions. I was afraid of having a baby. I had never been through anything like that. I felt good one moment and sick the next. Then I was afraid again. My mind and body were all mixed up. The joy of knowing that I was growing a baby inside of me made me feel so good. It was part of me. Wow, what a feeling. Then the sickness would start. I knew that morning sickness came along with pregnancy, but it sure didn't feel good. Then after the sickness came, the fear began. I was afraid because I didn't know what I was doing or how to handle it.

I was a seventeen-year-old girl who thought she was an adult. My name is Wanda Mae Rainey—well, Lindsey now. I'm Wanda Mae Lindsey, thanks to the eighteen-year-old man I married. I had been happily married for almost a year. I was also pregnant. My whole life, this was all I had ever dreamed about.

As a little girl growing up, all I wanted was to be a housewife and a mother. I spent hours and hours playing house. I would fix my little playhouse just the way I wanted it to look. Then I would change it all up to look different. I would pretend I had children, three to be exact. I would have two girls and a boy. I dreamed so many times of being a housewife and a mother. Now my dream was coming true—right at that very moment; it was really happening. I was a housewife, and I was about to become a mother. How much more of an adult could I become? But deep down inside, I felt like a scared little child. I married when I was sixteen. At that age, how could I be anything but a child?

I missed my mom and dad. They always made me feel safe. They were very strict, but I knew they loved me. We rarely went to church, so I didn't really know Jesus or his love. Maybe my parents wanted me to know Jesus, but it's hard to teach somebody something that you barely know yourself. As they grew older, they grew closer to the Lord. They became regulars at a little church not far from their home.

In 1954 we didn't have cell phones; we didn't even have a telephone. We lived in Burkburnett, Texas, a small town 260 miles from Brownfield, Texas, where my mom lived. Jobs were hard to come by at the time, so we had to move where my husband could find work. My mom might as well have been on the other side of the world from me. I really didn't care how far away she was because when I was afraid or sick, all I knew was that she was not there to take care of me. I suppose in my heart I knew I still was just a child. There was no way I was an adult. I wanted to be one, and at times I could act like one, but when I was afraid or sick, I knew I wasn't an adult. I would cry for my mom to come and hold me and tell me everything would be okay. I wanted her to tell me that this baby inside of me was going to be okay. Was I doing this right? Was I walking enough? Was I eating all the right things? Was my baby going to be healthy? *Please, Lord, let my baby be healthy.* Was I going to be okay?

I wanted her to do what she had done my whole life. I would get hurt, and she would come and fix it for me. When I was afraid, she would hold me and tell me it would be okay. When she held me in her arms, I felt so safe that the fear went away. That's what I wanted; I wanted my mom to come and hold me. But in 1954, in this situation, this was not possible. I couldn't simply go and ask her for her advice and her love. I missed her so much. I even missed her when I felt happy, but it was not as difficult to deal with.

3

When I felt happy, I was an adult again. The joy of knowing my dream was coming true made it all bearable. When I wasn't sick or afraid, which was less and less as time went on, I was the housewife and soon-to-be mother that I was when I played house as a child—only this time it wasn't playing. It was real. The thought of my dreams coming true made me feel so happy again until the fear and sickness returned. It was an emotional roller coaster.

This Halloween night was different from the rest. I had been feeling miserable for several weeks. I was in my ninth month of pregnancy. I don't think there was a single part of my body that was not swollen and stretched, especially my stomach. On this night, all the joy of the kids trick-or-treating made me feel so warm and good inside. But still, this night felt different. I did not know why I felt this way, but later on I would find out.

In 1954, we did not have the technology to tell if a baby was a boy or a girl. You just had to wait and see. I wondered what my baby was going to be. I really didn't care—I just wanted a baby. I did not even know when it was coming. I knew it was getting close, but I really didn't know when. Little did I know how close it really was. I also didn't know that this night would be different from any night I had ever spent in my whole life. I would grow up quickly that night. That night I would become an adult.

The pain was unbearable. I didn't know what was happening to my body. Then my water broke. Thank God, my husband, Larry Leon Lindsey, was there. We grabbed my things and away we went. I don't know who was more nervous—my husband or me. When we finally arrived at the hospital, the staff took me right in. My body was being stretched and twisted in ways I never thought possible. I had felt pain in my life but never like that. I was screaming at the top of my lungs. They didn't let my husband come into the delivery room.

I had always wanted a baby, but I never dreamed it would come with so much pain. The pain was coming faster and faster without stopping in between. Before it would hurt awhile, then it would stop. But now it didn't stop. I couldn't stand it any longer. All I could think was *Dear Lord, please get this baby out of me.* All I wanted was for the pain to stop. I didn't care how—I just wanted it to stop. I now know the punishment that Eve received when she ate of the tree of knowledge from which God said she could not eat. The Bible says in Genesis 3:16, "To the woman he said, I will make your pains in childbearing very severe; with painful labor you will give birth to children. Your desire will be for your husband, and he will rule over you."

Even though this Halloween there was no trick, there was a treat: the baby was out. The pain was bearable now. "Oh my God, oh my God, oh my God," I yelled when I heard it cry. The baby that had been growing inside me for nine months was now crying. There are no words to explain how I felt at that moment. Never in all my life has there been another moment when I felt like this. Tears were pouring down my face. I was crying, and my baby was crying. We were crying together. My baby was really crying. And I could not stop crying. But this time it was not a cry of pain; it was a cry of joy, pure, unbelievable *joy.*

The word *joy* couldn't compare to how I felt then. It was beyond joy. I can't come up with a word that describes how I felt at the time. I don't think the English dictionary has a word to explain how joyous and wonderful I felt. Then, ah ... ah ... ah ... then I started stuttering. I couldn't even talk, and just when I thought this feeling couldn't be topped, I saw my baby. The nurse was bringing this beautiful little baby to me. It was mine. It came from me. It did—it really did. And it was a girl, more beautiful than anything I had ever seen in my entire life.

The nurse put the baby in my arms. I was holding my beautiful, little baby girl. I had never felt such joy in all my life. All the pain that I had experienced that night went away when I had my little "Baby Sandra Sue" in my arms. *Did this beautiful little girl really come from me?* I thought. *Am I really a mother now?*

My dream, the one I'd had my whole life had really come true. I was a housewife and a mother. I had never felt so much love in my life as I did with the birth of my Baby Sandra Sue. I looked into her little eyes and saw a part of me in her. I felt her breath on my arm. I felt her warm body against mine. I never wanted to let her go. I wanted to hold my little baby girl forever. For such pain to turn into the best Joy I had ever had was beyond my understanding. For this miracle to come out of me had to be proof that there is a God.

This could only be a gift from my God. "Thank you, Jesus, for giving me this precious gift," I said. "I know I don't deserve it. But thank you, Lord." Is this how God loved us? My mom would tell me as I was growing up that God loves us more than anything. Is this what she was talking about? Was this kind of love God's kind of love? It was so powerful. The way I loved and felt for my Baby Sandra Sue, this child of mine, was different from anything I had felt before. I had never known love like this. I remember my mom telling me and me hearing at church that we all could be one of God's children. We all had a choice to make!

Well, all I could say was "Thank you, God, for my Baby Sandra Sue." How could anyone love more than this? Did God really love me more than I loved my baby? Did he? How could he? Was this possible? If what he did was true, giving up his son for me, I figured it could be possible that God loved me more than I loved my Baby Sandra Sue. If that was true, "Thank you, God, for loving me this much. Thank you."

So, I guess my pain was not just a Halloween trick but a treat from God himself. My Baby Sandra Sue was

the beginning.

CHAPTER 2

TOO FAST

The old saying that time flies by fast when you are having fun is so true. It did not take very long at all before my Baby Sandra Sue had beautiful, long, curly blond hair. Her eyes were hazel; they were just like the seasons and would change color depending on how I dressed her. This time it was not just playing house; it was much, much more. It was real. I loved dressing her up in pretty outfits and putting bows in her hair. She was so pretty.

We did not have much money, but you know what? It didn't matter. I gave her the best I could. I didn't need new clothes or new bows to be happy. All I needed was her, just her. I could make do with the rest of the things.

My baby girl looked beautiful in anything she wore. I loved being her mother. She was the most precious and beautiful girl I had ever seen. I'm sure that every mother thinks the same thing: that her baby is the most beautiful gift God has ever given. But I know that my baby truly was. I loved this little miracle from God more than anything in this world.

Time passed so fast, and then it happened again, my second miracle from God. It was a boy, and it had been one year and eight days since my first miracle, Baby Sandra Sue, was born. God was so good. We named him "Lewis Lenard," and he was just as precious as my first. He looked just like his dad and was named after him. Actually my baby boy was the fourth generation of "LLLs." His father, Larry Leon Lindsey, was so proud of him. I guess a man loves to have someone to carry his family name into the future. I had never seen a bigger smile on any man's face than I did on his dad's.

Fourteen months later, my third miracle happened. I had my third child, another baby girl. She was just as pretty and precious as the first two children. We named her Barbra Ann. My dream of being a mother of a boy and two girls had come true.

My children were growing up fast. I loved them all the same, but none were like my little Baby Sandra Sue. Well, she was my first. There is something special about your first. You never forget your first boyfriend. You never forget your first anything. All my kids were miracles from God, and I knew it.

Baby Sandra Sue became quite the little helper. It was as if she was another little mother. She helped me to take care of Lewis and Barbra. She was quite the busybody. Everywhere she went she just started talking to everyone. She knew no strangers.

When my Baby Sandra Sue was four years old, we moved back to where my mom and dad lived. We had lived there for almost six months, and Baby Sandra Sue was now five years old. How could this be that five years had passed since that Halloween night when I got the best treat of my life: my Baby Sandra Sue? Little did I know just how fast time would fly by and how fast things would change.

Then one of the most horrible things happened. Her daddy had a bad car accident. Another car had crossed over into his lane early one morning and struck his car head-on; he was killed instantly. Baby Sandra Sue and I cried and cried together. Her daddy was gone. I think Lewis and Barbra were too young to understand what had happened. But not her; she knew full well what had occurred. It was so hard for me to deal with it, and it was devastating to her. I didn't know if she would ever really get over it. I hoped she would, but I had my doubts. I knew that I would never really get over it, but I had to be strong for my kids.

As we all know, there will be ups and downs in our lives. It is how we learn to deal with these ups and downs that makes us who we are.

It was 1960, six years since my Baby Sandra Sue had been born. My, time goes by so fast. I had been at the local grocery store shopping, and I was in the meat department, trying to decide what the best deal was, when I looked up and noticed the most gorgeous man I had ever seen. He had the biggest smile on his face. He must have been lifting weights because his body was all muscle. My eyes sparkled, and I could feel a special attraction to him. He walked right up to me and introduced himself. He said, "My name is Curtis Bailey, and I think you are the most beautiful girl I have ever seen." He melted my heart. We started going out and spending every moment together when we were not working.

One of the things that impressed me most about him

was that when I explained to him that I had three kids, he could not have cared less. He said he loved kids. We were soon married and starting our life together. My new husband and I moved into a little house in Lamesa, Texas. My mom and dad lived only forty miles away in Brownfield.

Once again my dream had come true: I was pregnant and married. My fourth miracle was a little girl, Kathlane Kay. She was so beautiful. I thought that after having three children, I would lose the excitement and joy of seeing a new baby born, but that wasn't the case when I saw this fourth little miracle from God. I was becoming a specialist at having babies. Would four kids be enough? I guess only time would tell. I loved them all the same. But as I said, the first was very special.

Before I knew it, Baby Sandra Sue was in first grade. She was so smart. The teacher always said that she was such a good helper. Sometimes she would get into trouble though for trying to be the boss.

The school was just down the street from where we lived. Every morning I woke up my beautiful little girl and began playing house all over again. It was as if I were still a child. I dressed her all up, and she looked so pretty. All the kids on the block walked down the street to school together. I watched out the front door as she walked toward the school. I could see her beautiful, long, curly blond hair blowing in the wind. She was the most precious and beautiful child of the whole group. She would always tell me, "Momma, don't let everyone see you watching me. The other kids will tease me."

My new husband and I did not go to church. He was a heavy drinker. This did not bother me because he was

11

always happy and laughing when he drank beer. I did not realize that we were raising our kids surrounded by all the alcohol and partying, which would soon teach our kids to do the same. This is a part of my life that I am not proud of.

My mother-in-law did take the kids to a little Baptist church. My husband insisted that they go. He always wanted me to go with them, but I told him that if he wasn't going, I wasn't either. He did convince me to go several times with the kids and his mother, and I did feel guilty when the kids went and I didn't go. I knew from my mother, when I was growing up, that I should attend church.

Once again I was pregnant, so I guess that four was not enough. The Lord blessed me with one more miracle, another beautiful little girl. We named her Jana Mae. I now had four girls and one boy. The Lord had blessed me even though I didn't go to church like I should. God must be merciful because he gave me five miracles when I did not deserve any of them. I knew I should go to church; I just did not always do it. I did know who the Lord was. My mom had taught me about him, and I learned more on the few occasions I went to church with the kids. I just never really got to know him. He was somewhere out there in heaven, not here in front of me to see. It was hard to believe in something I couldn't see.

Baby Sandra Sue went to church as often as she could. She knew every person who went to that church. That's just the way she was. There were not going to be any strangers with her. She just walked right up to people and start talking to them. Everyone there knew her.

She became devoted to this little church and wanted to be baptized. So I decided I would get baptized with her.

I think she might have understood a little of what she was doing, but at seven years old, I'm not sure she understood completely. I know I didn't understand what I was doing, not really. We were so happy that day. How fast time had flown by.

I don't ever remember doing this when I was playing house as a child. But I can tell you this: I was so happy and filled with joy. This was a joy unlike any other. I guess whatever you do that has something to do with God gives you a special kind of joy, one that lasts a long time. I knew, well, I felt that at this time I was doing something special and good with my Baby Sandra Sue.

The next thing I knew, she liked boys. Had she really grown up that fast? It seemed like everything else she had ever done was all the way or nothing, and she had every boy in high school chasing after her. One night a boy named Thomas Durham came over to our house and met us and asked if he could take my Baby Sandra Sue on a date. *No, no way*, I thought, *she is not old enough to go on a date*. But then I began to think about my own life. I was fifteen when I started dating her daddy. So I allowed her to go on this date. Was she really fifteen years old? How did time pass so quickly? She had been just a baby and now she was fifteen years old.

It was 1969 and my little girl thought she was an adult. I did too when I was her age. She turned sixteen and married the first boy she had gone out with. I guess when she told me that he was special to her, she meant it. She was married and pregnant at sixteen. Was it my life all over again? Was my Baby Sandra Sue following in my footsteps? No, this couldn't be; she couldn't be a wife and mother. I knew she had played house just like I did. I just hoped she enjoyed playing house as much as I did.

Things were different now, but she could call me anytime she felt afraid or sick or happy. I would still be there for my Baby Sandra Sue. Even though she was a wife who was going to have a baby, she would always be my Baby Sandra Sue.

I was going to be a grandmother, and I was so excited about it. Some women get scared when they think about getting old and becoming a grandmother. But not me, I couldn't wait. I would have so much fun with this grandbaby of mine.

* * *

My Baby Sandra Sue was now the mother of two baby girls of her own. Time kept passing so fast. I wanted to slow down the clock of life, but I couldn't. Time does not slow down or stop. I figured I had better learn to use my time a lot better because it would not stop and I couldn't go back and change it.

It was 1973 and I was working a lot for the telephone company. My baby boy, Lewis, was my babysitter. He watched the two little girls, Kathlane and Jana, while I was at work. He had become quite the little helper. I guess he learned from his older sister, Sandra Sue. My second daughter, Barbra, was fifteen years old and had met the love of her life.

The man of her dreams, Jason Weaver, lived just down the country road from where we lived. They met at the little country school in Balmorhea, Texas. It was there that her dreams began. There was no doubt that they belonged together. They spent every minute they could together. She would be right beside him in his old pickup. You could not get a toothpick between them. It was not long before they were married. Then her husband joined the US Army and off he went to begin a new life. Barbra stayed at home until he finished training, and then off she went too. They were so happy.

I was at work one day when my husband called, and what he said to me was difficult to deal with. He said, "Baby Sandra Sue's husband has been involved in an accident. I'm on my way to the hospital. It's very serious. You need to get Baby Sandra Sue and meet me at the hospital."

I began to panic. My Baby Sandra Sue's husband and daddy of my grandkids had been involved in an accident at work. Was he going to be okay? I picked up my daughter and away we went to the hospital, some thirty miles away.

Her husband was a mechanic on a road construction crew. A machine that he was working on blew up on him and his helper, who died at the scene, The fire was a diesel fire, a very hot fire. My son-in-law had third-degree burns all over his body. He looked horrible; his head was swelled up, maybe twice the size it normally was. His arms and chest looked horrible too. A burn is the most painful thing there is.

He stayed almost a year at the burn center. My Baby Sandra Sue stayed with him and helped take care of him. He recovered from this accident with scars, both emotional and physical.

* * *

After a few years had passed, the unthinkable happened again. My Baby Sandra Sue went to the hospital to have her third baby. It was a boy, the boy that she and her husband had always wanted. We were going to call him Skeet. Yes, that would be his nickname.

There were complications when he was born. His heart was not functioning properly, and sadly, at just eleven *hours* old, my grandson's heart stopped beating and Skeet died. This was the third big tragedy that had happened so far in my Baby Sandra Sue's life—the death of her daddy, her husband's accident, and now the death of her only son. It was more than she could handle. Even though her son was so young and hadn't been on this earth very long, it still had to be a great tragedy for her. I knew that she would never really recover from this one. I can't even begin to imagine how she felt. You could see the pain in her eyes. This was my grandson so it was unbearable for me too. I knew it had to be for her. But we did not have a choice; we had to go on for the rest of the kids.

I asked myself, *Is this how God felt when he gave his son to die for us?* It hurt my heart so much when Skeet died. Did God hurt like this when his only son died? God made the choice to let his son die a horrible death so we could go to heaven and be with him. Did God really love me that much? Did he love everyone on this earth that much? This kind of love is unbelievable. There is no way I could ever give up one of my kids for anyone. I did not make the choice to let Skeet die. I couldn't do that. I guess God really did love us so much that he gave his son to die for us.

I was working more now, and it was becoming harder and harder to spend time with my Baby Sandra Sue and her two baby girls. She had a life of her own now, and we were both busy.

We all got together several times a year. Thanksgiving was a special time for our entire family to be together. All my kids and their kids would come to my house. Lewis was married and had two boys. Barbra Ann was married and had three girls. Kathlane Kay was married and had two boys of her own and two girls from her husband's previous marriage. Jana Mae was married and also had two girls. There was always a lot of drinking and partying happening on these occasions. We did not act like godly people at all during these times. I don't think any of us went to church at this period in our lives. We were too busy partying to get to know the Lord. It became longer and longer between visits but not because we stopped loving or caring about each other. The world was just moving

too fast.

CHAPTER 3

THE CHANGE:
JESUS FREAKS

The partying grew worse and worse. Every time the kids came for a visit, partying is all we cared about, so that's what we did. It seemed like so much fun. There was always laughing and joking. Most of the jokes should never have been told, but we told them anyway and drank and partied. It was what we had become: party animals. Doesn't that sound fun?

It was fun until one of us got too drunk. It didn't happen all the time, but when it did, it was bad. When it turned bad, there was always a big fight, which ruined our laughing and joking. My son, Lewis, was the worst.

He was married and had two kids. He had spent time in the army and now was working for a construction company with his stepdad. He could not hold his liquor at all. When he got drunk, he always got angry with someone and started a fight. I think he was doing a lot more than drinking. I think he was getting into drugs too. I wasn't sure, but the way he acted when he got drunk seemed like he was consuming more than just alcohol.

Once, at a family reunion at Lake Brownwood, Lewis drank too much and started cussing at his wife. It made everyone get angry with him. He didn't care; he was drunk and whatever else he was doing. He jumped in the car and tried to drive, but we convinced him to let his wife drive. He went around to the passenger's door, got into the car, and fell into the bowl of potato salad he was taking home. It was so sad to be raising two boys this way.

We thought we were having so much fun, and as long as things didn't go bad, we were. But when things went bad and the fights started, I did not know whose side to take. They were all my kids. I loved them all the same. It was horrible to try to stop them when they began to fight.

Many times I was the problem, drunk and right in the middle of the fight or starting it. We screamed, cussed, slapped, punched, and just about anything else you could think of that was immoral or bad. It was as if we died and went to hell. When I got up the next morning, I would feel so sick and embarrassed and ashamed. A lot of the time I didn't even remember what I did. I guess I was not that sick though because the next day I usually was drinking again and laughing about being sick. All of us did this. We cried in the morning when we woke up, but it wasn't long before we were drinking all over again. Sometimes we never went to bed at all; we just drank all night and did not stop.

I knew this lifestyle was not right. I also knew that if things didn't change, it would all end up in disaster. We were living for the devil, and the devil loved it.

My mother and dad never drank. I was not raised to

drink or party the way I was now. I never drank growing up, nor did I do any partying then. I never drank a beer or any alcohol until I was twenty-two years old.

I knew, at forty-two years of age, that the drinking was slowly taking charge of my life. Every weekend, all we did was drink and drink and drink some more. We couldn't wait for weekends. When my kids came down, that's all we would do. The fights occurred more and more often. The embarrassment and shame soon became resentment. Then, as soon as everyone drank enough, that resentment turned into anger and the fights began again.

The fun was slowly leaving our get-togethers. I'm not sure what my kids did when they went home on Sunday or what they did when they didn't come down on the weekends. I'm pretty sure they did the same thing. Were we becoming alcoholics? What had I taught my kids to do?

Then it happened again. I got a call at 5:15 a.m. on June 21, 1988. It was about my son, Lewis. He had been working out of town on a construction job. He had been in an accident and wrecked his pickup. The call was from his wife, and she said I needed to get to the hospital. She had received a call from the highway patrol saying that Lewis had been in a wreck and was on his way to the hospital in critical condition. His wife was leaving to drive there.

I loaded up the car and drove to the hospital. This was my only boy. The trip was awful because I didn't know if he was going to be okay or not. Was it going to be like his dad? I was so afraid I was going to lose my son like my Baby Sandra Sue lost her boy, like I lost my grandson. No, I couldn't handle this, not my son. I cried all the way there. I thought I was going to have a nervous breakdown.

I finally arrived at the hospital after driving for an hour and a half. I jumped out of the car—I hoped I had parked it right; well, I really didn't care—and ran into the hospital. No one else was there yet. Lewis's wife had to drive three hours to get there. I asked every nurse I saw about my son. Then the doctor came out and told me that he was going to be okay. He was lucky. He rolled over his pickup three times. Although Lewis would live, his lower back had been broken, and the doctor told me he might never walk again. He had also broken three ribs on his left side, two ribs on his right side, and his wrist. He was cut up and bruised pretty badly, but he would live. I stayed at the hospital with my son and his wife.

The doctor said that his blood test showed his alcohol level was double the legal limit and he'd had marijuana and methamphetamines in his system. So he *was* doing more than just drinking. What we had suspected was true. I hated it. I thought it was always someone else's kid, not my kid. No, it couldn't be my kid. I never had been around drugs, but I was sure that drugs were very addicting because I knew how addicting drinking was. What was happening to my family? Had the disaster I feared finally arrived?

My job had called me so I needed to return home once my son stabilized. I could only take off for so long. This was a great tragedy for me. My son was never going to walk again. His wife stayed with him, and she called me a few days after I got home. She was in shock; she could barely talk. She told me that my son said, "Someone came into the hospital room and told me that God sent him there to tell me that if I did not change my life and get close to God, God was going to let me die." My son's wife did not see this guy come in the room, and no one else saw him either. Lewis said he prayed with this guy right then and asked God to help him get his life close to God. Could this have happened? Was it really true? Was there such a thing as a real angel, and did a real angel come to save my son?

It had to be real. It was not just a dream *because my son was walking.* As the angel was leaving the room, my son got up out of bed and started to walk. He really did. Yes, it's true. The doctors could not believe it. My daughter-in-law could not believe it. I could not believe it either. This had to be a miracle from God. I'm not sure which miracle was better, my son being born or his back being healed. I only know that God keeps giving me miracles. I know that I do not deserve them, especially after the life I had been living.

This really scared me. The doctors had told me that Lewis would never be able to walk and here he was walking. I remembered that my son had told me that he asked Jesus into his heart when he was sixteen years old. And I even got baptized with my Baby Sandra Sue several years earlier. I knew that I had felt God then, but now this feeling truly was God. No one else could have done this. My son was walking. Even the doctors said it was a miracle.

My daughter-in-law told me the doctor had released him and they were going home. My son was still beat up and cut up with broken ribs and a broken wrist, but his back was healed. My son became totally sold on Jesus. He was not like those religious people who condemned you for every little thing you did wrong. He said that Jesus loved him and he loved us too.

Lewis said that the biggest miracle was not his back being healed but what Jesus had taken away from him.

What did Jesus really take away? He took the addiction to hard drugs away from him. He took away the addiction to smoking marijuana. My son said he had been smoking two packs of cigarettes a day. But now he quit smoking anything. God not only took away these bad habits, but he also took away the desire for these things. Thank you, Jesus.

Lewis truly felt God's love inside him, and his life was radically changed. Things changed around my house too. My son still came to my house almost every weekend, but he was totally a different person. He kept talking about Jesus and how much Jesus loved us. We all kept drinking and partying, but he didn't. He didn't scold us or condemn us. He said Jesus would take care of that, and he didn't have to do that. It wasn't his job to judge us. His job was to tell us how much Jesus loved us. He kept telling us that Jesus only wanted what was best for us if we would learn to hear his voice and do as he asked us to do. We then would have a peace that would last forever. He said he knew it was hard for anyone to understand how much Jesus loved us, but he had faith that Jesus would help us to understand in time.

This was different from what I had heard at church while growing up. The church services made me feel that Jesus wouldn't love me if I didn't stop sinning and start doing everything right. That was not what my son said. He said Jesus would love me no matter what I did. He said what made heaven so good was that there was no sin there. You could not get into heaven if you had sin in your life. He also said that everyone on earth had sin. He showed me Romans 3:23, which said, "For all have sinned and fall short of the glory of God."

I asked him how someone got into heaven then. Lewis

said that was why Jesus came to earth. He was tempted, but he never sinned. Instead He died on the cross to pay for our sins. If I would just let him into my heart and believe that he died on the cross to take away our sins, I would no longer have any sins; I would go to heaven and be with God in paradise. He said that Jesus could see our hearts and tell if we really believed or not. So we really had to believe that he paid for our sins; if we didn't, our prayers would not mean anything. My son said he was going to keep praying for us.

As time went by, each one of us began to accept what my son was saying. Lewis was so passionate about his Jesus that it made me want to have what he had. There was something special about how he acted. What was it? I couldn't figure it out. I just knew my son was at peace with himself. His face was shining all the time now. He always had this big, happy smile on his face.

One Thanksgiving when we were all gathered around, my son began to tell us all about his life and what he had been through. You could have heard a pin drop once he started telling his story. Everyone wanted to know what it was that could change a person so drastically. My son said he had been drinking a lot and involved in drugs. He said that after a while he could not afford to buy the drugs, so he had to start selling them too. That's the only way he could afford them. Eventually he began doing hard drugs because weed and drinking no longer satisfied him. Once he got to that point, all he cared about was the next high. Every penny he could come up with or steal he would spend on drugs. He said that he became so addicted that nothing else mattered—not his family, not his kids, not anything but the next high.

Lewis said he couldn't understand how his life could change so radically because of drugs, not until all this happened to him and he looked back on his life. Jesus showed him that he did all this because he felt empty inside. He tried to fill his heart with all kinds of stuff, drugs, alcohol, and sex. These things made him feel okay for a while, or maybe all they did was numb his feelings.

I think there are many of us who have pain from tragedy in our life, and we don't know how to deal with it. So we just push it down, deep down in ourselves, so we don't have to deal with it. The only problem is that it makes us feel so empty inside. Then it keeps popping up every time we see something that reminds us of the problem.

The stuff we put in our hearts only works for a short while. It worked for Lewis for a shorter and shorter amount of time. Then the empty feeling in his heart would come back, and he would have to do something stronger each time to numb his heart. He was never at peace with himself. He said that's how he felt until that angel came into his room at the hospital and prayed with him. Jesus filled that empty feeling in his heart, and he no longer needed drinking or drugs to feel his heart.

Lewis said Jesus wanted to be in our hearts, so he could help us too. He loved us so much that he only wanted what was best for us. This was starting to make since to me. I knew there was something different about Lewis. He was always happy and at peace now. He kept saying that the biggest miracle was not that Jesus healed his back but that he took away all Lewis's addictions. He told us he had no desire to do hard drugs again. He said that Jesus took all the brokenness that he'd had in his life and turned it into love. Jesus took away the alcohol; he didn't need it anymore. Jesus filled the emptiness inside his heart with love. His only desire was to tell people what Jesus had done for him and that he wanted to do the same thing for all of us.

I thought that wreck had been a horrible disaster, and I never wanted it to happen again. But somehow Jesus has a way of turning all our disasters and all our horrible things into something good and beautiful. I know that Jesus loves me so much and that I am important and precious to him. Jesus dying on the cross to pay for my sins proves this to me. Several years have passed now and several prayers have been spoken, and I can now say with confidence that Jesus used that wreck to reach everyone in our family and that they have all accepted Jesus into their hearts.

All four of my daughters, my son, my husband, and I are going to spend eternity together with Jesus in heaven. We are no longer "party animals"; we are

Jesus freaks.

CHAPTER 4

THE WRECK

It was 2011 and many years had passed. I was growing old. I didn't want to grow old, but one thing I had learned was that you cannot stop Father Time. He will keep ticking no matter how bad you want him to stop. There had been many times over the past seventy-five years when I wanted to stop Father Time. Then there had been others when I wanted him to speed up.

At seventy-five years old, my body was old and worn out. I had replaced both knees, and I needed to have my shoulder replaced too. But after my knees, my shoulder would have to get a lot worse before I went through that again. It was getting harder and harder to make my body do what I wanted it to. I hated getting old because my body didn't work as well as it used to. But, on the other hand, I loved getting older because I knew as each day passed I was getting one day closer to seeing my Jesus.

I was now known as "Mema." I had lost my husband, who was known as "Pepa." I knew he was in heaven now. Lewis came over a few days before Pepa's death and asked him, "If you died right now, do you know where you would go?" Pepa quickly said, "I know I am going to heaven because when I was younger, I asked Jesus into my heart and I meant it with all my heart." So my son said, "Mema, I know that Pepa will be waiting for you when you arrive in heaven."

This made my son and me feel so good deep inside our hearts.

I knew that Pepa was with my Baby Sandra Sue's son, Skeet, whom we lost at the age of eleven hours. I told Lewis, "I am so jealous of Pepa because I want to see Skeet again myself, and I know Pepa is spending time with him right now."

I know that when you talk about eternity, it means forever. I will get to spend eternity with my husband and with Skeet. I will never lose them again. It will be so wonderful because all of their sins and all my sins will not be there to hurt them or me. Sin only causes hurt and pain for me or the ones I love.

I guess that is why God tells us not to sin. He gives us a choice whether to sin or not; it is our choice. We will not be able to sin with our resurrected bodies when we get to heaven. The best part of heaven is that you will not be able to sin and hurt anyone and no one will be able to sin and hurt you. We will only be able to *love* one another.

Losing a grandchild and a husband was so tragic. I felt so empty inside when I lost my grandchild because he was so young, and then my husband. I know that I will see him when I get to heaven. Knowing this and that Skeet is in heaven has brought me peace. Can you imagine what heaven might be like for a child? I think Disney World would be heaven for a child, but that is man-made. What kind of playground is Skeet playing on right now? God created the whole world just by speaking words. Can you imagine what kind of a playground he created in heaven for the children to play on?

I know that my Baby Sandra Sue never was able to deal with Skeet's death. I can't imagine how she felt; it had to have been so tragic for her. She tried to act tough, but we all knew it almost drove her insane. Sometimes I think it took her across the line and she was insane for a while and then somehow she stepped back and was able to deal with it.

That year Baby Sandra Sue got involved in a little church again. It had been a long time since she had gone to church; it was at this time I noticed that her life had changed. She was no longer bitter. She and her husband became very involved in this little church. Now it was finally complete. All five of my children had Jesus in their lives and were involved in church one way or another.

My, how Jesus used my son and the wreck, which we thought was such a disaster, to save my whole family. The way we were living before the wreck was totally devoted to Satan, but now there is no doubt we are living for Jesus. We still sin and fall way short of what we are supposed to do, but Jesus takes care of all that. We are free in Jesus.

By 2011 I had raised five children and had sixteen, well, counting Skeet, seventeen grandchildren. I had twenty-one great-grandchildren and one great-great-grandchild. I lived in a cute little house that my son, Lewis, built for me. He lived just down the road and came by almost every day. He said it was to eat, but I knew he really wanted to see his mom. He was divorced now. There was no one in his life, at least not a girl he was serious about. Maybe that's why he came by. He tried to act tough, so he kept saying it was the food, but I'm his mom and I knew better.

His daughter, Dawn, one of my seventeen grandchildren, still lived with him. She was engaged. After she got married, it would be just Lewis and me on this road.

* * *

My Baby Sandra Sue and two of her granddaughters, two of my twenty-one great-grandchildren, came to visit me one day. One of them was born on my birthday. I remember when Kathy, one of the two girls visiting, was born sixteen years ago; my how fast time had flown by. We were all at the hospital, and my son came to Kathy's birth. He brought me a pineapple and said, "I was going to send you to Hawaii for your birthday, but I couldn't afford it, so I brought you a pineapple so you would think you were in Hawaii." He was always funny like that.

Baby Sandra Sue and her two granddaughters arrived at my house at about one o'clock on Tuesday, July 17, 2012. My son stopped by as usual. He aggravated the two girls as he always did. We were talking about taking the two girls shopping for clothes, and my son told them about a used clothing store. This place was like heaven to teenage girls. There were all kinds of clothes and shoes and purses and jewelry. They were all used, but they were name brands. They had been expensive when they were new, but here they were cheap and still like new.

My son told the two girls if they waited till his daughter, Dawn, got off work at five o'clock the next afternoon, she would go with them. She knew right where to go and could show them around the store. She had been there many times.

The next day, July 18, was very hot and the sun was beating down that morning. I don't think it ever cooled down all night long. It was already ninety degrees outside. The two girls arose early. The heat never fazed them at all. They were dressed and bugging their grandmother, my Baby Sandra Sue, and me, their great-grandmother, better known as Mema. They said, "Get ready, Mema, and let's go. Hurry; let's go."

They were so excited about going shopping. I guess all teenage girls get excited when they get to go shopping for clothes. Kathy, my sixteen-year-old great-granddaughter was so beautiful. She had blond hair, and her face was so pretty and soft looking. Her birthday was the same as mine, May 29. Miranda was my thirteen-year-old great-granddaughter. She was also beautiful with pretty brown hair. Miranda was the shy one, but I could tell she was excited about going shopping.

We left about ten-thirty that Wednesday morning. The girls were too excited to wait for anyone to get off work. They wanted to wait for Dawn, but it was impossible; they just couldn't wait. We went in my van so there would be plenty of room, and my Baby Sandra Sue drove. I didn't like driving when there was a lot of traffic.

I could hear Kathy and Miranda in the backseat talking about what they were going to look for. I could see the big smile on Baby Sandra Sue's face as she listened to them. She had given them money for shopping, and so did I. I wanted them to have fun, so it was worth it. The old saying "It is better to give than receive" was true this day, especially for me. The big smile on the faces of Baby Sandra Sue and my two great-granddaughters was more valuable than any amount of money.

We laughed and laughed the entire thirty-one miles to the used clothing store. To the girls it seemed like hours; we couldn't get there fast enough. They kept asking, "How much farther is it? Are we almost there?"

We arrived at the store at 11:10 a.m. We parked three parking spaces away from the front door. The girls' door flew open and out they jumped. It was so hot that they immediately began to sweat. I think you could have fried an egg on the sidewalk outside the store. I'm not sure if it was the heat of the scorching sun or the excitement of shopping that made them sweat so much. The two girls were saying once again, "Come on, Mema. Hurry; get out. We want to go inside. Hurry, Mema, hurry."

My Baby Sandra Sue was so happy to see her two granddaughters so excited and happy. I was happy for them also, and seeing my Baby Sandra Sue so happy made me feel so good inside.

We all went inside, and the girl's eyes grew big. They couldn't believe what they saw. The place was full of name-brand clothes, shoes, purses, and jewelry and at a price they could afford. You should have watched those girls go after it. They were like pros shopping and trying on clothes and shoes. I heard it a million times: "Mema, how does this look on me?" Then they would turn to my Baby Sandra Sue, whom they called "Nana," and say all over again, "Nana, how does this look on me?"

I even saw Nana looking at things she liked. She told me to look at a purse, and if I liked it, she would get it for me. I think she really wanted the purse for herself. I didn't want a purse, but I told myself I would get one, and when Baby Sandra Sue left, I would give it to her. We were all having so much fun.

The girls were going in and out of the dressing rooms, trying on different clothes. They were in heaven. I think my Baby Sandra Sue was also in heaven watching her granddaughters. We were there for an hour and a half.

We left with a big bag full of our favorite clothes. We were all so happy on the drive back. Kathy and Miranda were telling each other how much they liked what they got and when they were going to wear them and where. My Baby Sandra Sue was delighted that her two babies were so happy. And I was so pleased with my new purse.

It was about two o'clock and we were heading back to my house. Baby Sandra Sue, who was driving, said, "It's happy hour. Let's stop and get something to drink." The girls didn't even hear her because they were so busy looking at and talking about their clothes. She said again, "It's happy hour at Sonic. Let's stop and get something to drink." Kathy finally said, "Sure, let's stop; that sounds good." I was laughing at them. I was not sure I had ever seen two teenage girls so elated.

We stopped and got cherry limeades. While we were there, I felt God was talking to me. I really wasn't sure why God wanted me to do this at first, but later I would know beyond a shadow of a doubt that it was God at work in my life. He told me to put a few things in that new purse. So, while we were sitting at Sonic, I took my ID and insurance cards and put them in that new purse along with my cell phone. I noticed that it showed my last call, which had been to my other daughter, Jana. That's all I put in the purse. I set it down right beside my seat and put my old purse in the backseat.

Baby Sandra Sue was so excited that she called her

husband. She told him what we had done and how overjoyed the two girls were. They shared everything with each other. I'm not sure if any of my other kids were as close to their spouses as these two were. They really cared for and wanted to spend time with each other. I think they were a good example of how God wanted two married people to treat each other. They talked awhile, and then we pulled out onto the highway. We made it about three miles down the highway before it happened––another tragedy.

I looked up and I saw a black pickup heading right for us. I hollered, "Sandra, they're going to hit us." I'm not sure she had time to react. The next thing I knew I heard what sounded like the scraping of metal. It was a loud and shrill sound. It was almost like the sound of scratching a chalkboard. It seemed like it lasted forever. It made the hair on my neck stand up.

Then it was as if time jumped ahead because I could hear both of the girls screaming, "Where is my sister? Where is my sister?" They kept screaming it over and over. I couldn't move. I know I was conscious, but I couldn't move. It was as if I was in a dream, but I knew I wasn't. I knew this was real. I heard it over and over again, the horrible sound of both of the girls screaming, "Where is my sister? Where is my sister?" All I could do was ask Jesus to help us. Then suddenly I felt a cloud cover the two girls, and they quit screaming. I knew it was the hand of Jesus; I knew he had put his hand over them and held them. It had to be.

I couldn't move, but I didn't know why. Was I paralyzed? What was wrong with me? Then I don't know if my Baby Sandra Sue had just awoken or if I just now heard her for the first time. It was a horrible scream; I had never heard anything like it in my life. Baby Sandra Sue was screaming in a pleading voice. "Please, please, please help me. Please, anyone, help me." She kept screaming over and over, "Please, please, someone help me. Please help me."

I couldn't see her. I don't know why I couldn't see her or the two girls. Was I blind? Why couldn't I see them? My daughter was begging me to help her, and all I could do was hear her scream and cry. I couldn't move. I tried so hard to help her. I tried so hard. I kept telling my body to help her, but my body wouldn't move. I couldn't feel any pain in my body, but I could feel my Baby Sandra Sue's pain because she was screaming so loud over and over. All I could do was sit and let her suffer. I wanted to help her so badly that I could feel the tears rolling down my face. I thought my heart was going to break from hearing my Baby Sandra Sue suffer so much and not being able to do anything to help her.

Then I heard a lot of voices, and I didn't hear my Baby Sandra Sue screaming anymore. I'm not sure if they gave me something or if they gave her something, or both of us. But the screaming had stopped. This made me so happy. She was no longer screaming. I could see them moving her out of the car; there was blood everywhere. I could see my Baby Sandra Sue now. Her waist had a big cut from one side of her body to the other. It was very deep. They were trying to stop the bleeding, My poor, poor Baby Sandra Sue was hurt and in so much pain. I don't remember anything else. Was this all a dream? No, it wasn't a dream, as bad as I wanted it to be. I knew for sure that this was a

wreck.

CHAPTER 5

DEATH OF
MY SISTER

My name is Lewis Lenard. Baby Sandra Sue is my older sister. It was around three o'clock in the afternoon when I received a call from my sister Barbra, who was on her way to visit Mema. The words she spoke to me caused me to lose my breath. My heart started beating hard. It was thumping so hard and fast that I thought it was going to bust my chest wide open. I began to sweat and panic. Yes, panic. I thought I was the strong one of our family, but at this moment in time, all my strength left me. I was not the strong one anymore.

Barbra said, "Jana just called me, and Mom and Sandra and the two girls have been involved in a car accident." Barbra was very upset and in a panic as she began to explain to me what Jana had said.

She had told Barbra, "I just received a call from a highway patrolman. The patrolman said, 'Do you know Wanda Bailey?' I said, 'Yes, she is my mother.' The patrolman said, 'Wanda Bailey and Sandra Durham and two young girls have been involved in a car accident. Wanda and Sandra are in critical condition. The two girls have been injured, but they are not in critical condition. They are being taken to the hospital.' The highway patrolman said he got Mema's cell phone out of her purse and called the last number that she had called on her cell phone. The last call was to me."

After talking to the patrolman, Jana had immediately called Barbra, but she was crying and could barely get her words out.

This was just another act of God being at work in Baby Sandra Sue's and Mema's life. It could only have been God telling Baby Sandra Sue to buy the new purse for Mema at the store and Mema putting her ID and her cell phone in the new purse at the Sonic, and leaving it where they could find it so easily.

I then called Dawn, my daughter, and she met me at the office and away we went. I called Ashley, my secretary and very dear friend. I considered her to be one of my daughters. When I told her what had happened, she said she was on her way back from picking up parts for work, and the police had closed off the highway and made her go the back way home. She had no idea that it was Mema in the accident.

I had to decide if I should go the back way or take a chance on the traffic being cleared out by now. I decided to stay on the highway and hope I could get through quickly. There was still traffic backed up, but it was moving at a slow pace. It seemed like hours getting through the traffic; however, it was only for about two miles and then the pace picked, and my daughter and I made a beeline for the hospital. I didn't wait for the traffic lights to change; if it was clear, I stepped on the gas. The speed limit signs meant nothing to me. I guess you could say I was still in a panic. My daughter kept telling me, "Dad, slow down or you're not going to make it there. You are going to be in an accident too." Dawn finally told me in a very loud and harsh voice, "Dad, if you don't slow down, our chances of getting there are very slim." If not for her being there, we might have had another wreck.

We arrived at the hospital safely. I don't know how, the way I was driving. We were told that Baby Sandra Sue had been taken to another hospital but that Mema and the two girls were there.

I went into a room where Kathy was being treated. They were cleaning up a deep cut on her forehead. It was ugly and gross. It made me sick to my stomach. I didn't like blood or open cuts or anything like that. She also had a broken arm and a broken leg.

My sister Barbra came into the room and said, "I was on my way to Mema's house to visit her. I drove up on the wreck and started complaining about having to wait for the traffic to clear out. I wanted to get to Mema's house. I had no idea that it was Mema in the wreck. I saw them loading the car on the tow truck and thought that it looked like Mema's van. But I thought, no, it couldn't be her van."

I guess God is at work in places even when we don't even know it. Barbra was able to turn around and get to the hospital quickly because God placed her at the accident. That is just too wild. It could only be Jesus.

I went into Miranda's room to check on her. She had a bad cut on her leg that they were sewing up. She also had a chipped bone in her hip.

My mother, Mema, was in surgery, and I was told it

would be a while before they would know anything. My sister Baby Sandra Sue was at another hospital. We all wondered why they took her there. We kept calling to check on her, but no one would tell us anything. So Dawn and I decided to go to the hospital where Sandra was.

When we arrived there, Baby Sandra Sue's husband, my brother-in-law, had just arrived. The preacher from our church, and a longtime friend of the family and member of our church, had been there for a little while. A few minutes after we arrived Ashley and her husband, Joe, arrived and met us. They brought Dawn's boyfriend with them.

We were all in the waiting room talking when Baby Sandra Sue's husband told us that the doctor had just come out and said they had just sewn her up. Her liver had been cut almost in half. She also had a compound fracture of her right ankle. The doctor said she was still losing blood and they were trying to determine where it was coming from. What happened next would change my world and everyone's world around me forever. My family's world would never be the same again. My brother-in-law's life would be turned upside down.

The doctor came through the double doors that led to the operating room and what he told us was unbelievable. He walked up to my brother-in-law, looked him straight in the eyes, and said, "Sandra didn't make it." He said they had to go back in and try to stop her liver from bleeding, and when they did, her heart gave way and stopped beating. They tried everything they could to get her heart to start beating again, but it just gave out. The doctor said, "I am so sorry. I did everything I could. I just could not save her."

The painful look in her husband's eyes was devastating.

He just kept saying over and over, "This is not good. This is not good." His face turned white. I have never seen anyone look as lost as he did. He had just lost the love of his life after forty-two years together. They were closer to each other than any of my other sisters were with their husbands. All I could do was to lay hands on him. We all did. God showed himself again as our preacher had been placed there to lead us in a prayer. He called us all together to pray for Baby Sandra Sue's husband and lay hands on him. There were no words to say to make things better.

I got my brother-in-law's cell phone and found his daughter's cell number on his phone. I hit call, and it started ringing. What was I going to say to her? Her mother had just died. What can you say? I shut my eyes and asked Jesus to help me say it right. When she answered, I said, "Your mom didn't make it." She said, "What?" I said, "Listen to me. Sandra didn't make it; she has gone to heaven." All I could hear was her screaming and crying. I hated this, but I had to tell her.

Sometimes we need to learn from Job's friends in the Bible, who, in the book of Job, just sat with Job for one week without saying a word. This gave Job comfort simply knowing they were there. They didn't have to say anything. What could I say to my brother-in-law that would make him feel better? I could only stand with him and hold him. I don't think he even believed it. I know I didn't believe it. I still don't. I know it's true, but I still can't accept it. I know it will take him a lot longer to accept that she is gone. This had to be a bad nightmare.

We were told that we could go in and see her in a few minutes and say good-bye. So we waited in disbelief. All

I could do was try to make myself believe that this really had happened and that it was not a nightmare—a horrible, horrible nightmare.

After a few moments, the nurse led us into her room. Her husband, Dawn, and I went in to see her. She looked so pale. Her husband immediately touched her face and started crying. "This is not supposed to happen," he said. "I'm going to miss you. I love you so much." The pain on his face was awful. I wanted to cry when I saw him hurting so much. He looked lost. I said good-bye to Sandra, and Dawn said good-bye to her. It was so hard. Inside I kept waiting for her to open her eyes and start talking to me. I just couldn't believe she was gone. It hurt so much inside my heart because I knew she was really gone. Her husband kept touching her face, caressing her cheeks, and playing with her hair as if he was trying to see if she was really gone.

It was so sad that she had to leave us like that. I knew she was in heaven now. I didn't like it because we were going to miss her so much. Things can change so fast in life. You never know when your time has come. It was Baby Sandra Sue's time to go. It was so hard for me to accept the

death of my sister.

CHAPTER 6

OUR LAST CONVERSATION

My name is Lenard. Lewis is my dad. Baby Sandra Sue was my aunt. The last time I talked with my aunt Sandra it was the greatest conversation we'd ever had. She told me a story filled with pain, sadness, hope, and love. Sitting on a porch swing on Mema's front porch, which overlooked a tranquil pond, we watched the horses eating lush green grass and slid into another time and place as she began to reveal the very depths of her past misery.

Aunt Sandra said she married her husband at an early age; she had found the love of her life. She was chasing her dream until she woke up in his arms. Her heart was elated. Her future promised endless love from a prince who made her feel like a princess, right out of the pages of a fairy tale. As we all know, along with dreams come nightmares, and my aunt Sandra told me about hers.

Her husband was driving to a job site so he could perform maintenance on some equipment. He had a partner who rode with him and helped him out. They had just finished putting a new fuel filter in a pneumatic roller so it needed to be primed in order to start. Back then they used an oxygen tank to push the fuel to the filters. This was a quick and easy way to get the equipment primed so it would start up again without any trouble. If only they knew what was about to take place. Under very precise conditions, this method could create enough pressure for combustion to take place. On this particular day, the temperature, the ratio of the chemicals in the mixture, the pressure, and the sequence were just right for the fuel to ignite. The fire wouldn't have been so bad if it hadn't been for the open tank of oxygen. But this combination created a mass of flames so hot that the wrench my uncle's helper was holding melted right in his hand. Aunt Sandra's husband and his partner were engulfed in flames. His partner died instantly, and my uncle, Sandra's husband and holder of her heart, was in critical condition with third-degree burns over 65 percent of his body. Sandra clung to a flicker of hope that the small spark of life that remained in her husband would arise and come back to hold her once again. She wasn't prepared for her dream to be so suddenly extinguished by this merciless inferno.

After Aunt Sandra spent many agonizing days in the hospital beside the love of her life, her husband woke up by the grace of God! She was so glad to see him alive though unrecognizable and extensively bandaged. As she told me the ending of her story, she looked into my eyes and expressed how grateful she was to God for saving her husband, the love of her life. She confessed how blessed she was to have such a wonderful man for so many years and how happy each day of her life had been married to her soul mate.

This is the first time I have revealed the story of the

last time Aunt Sandra and I spoke. I hope one day to share this with my uncle. I hope it lifts his spirits, though it may bring tears to us both. I also hope to one day find what my aunt and uncle found in one another. I want to cherish each day I spend with my loved ones and be thankful for the gifts God has shared with me during this short time on earth. God bless you, Aunt Sandra! I want to thank you for sharing with me

our last conversation.

CHAPTER 7

HEAVEN OR HELL

I, Mema, woke up and was lost. Where was I? What happened to me? I didn't know where I was. I was hooked up to all kinds of tubes and lines. There was a ventilator tube and a feeding tube. There were beeping sounds. Was I ... was I in the hospital? It looked like a hospital room and a hospital bed. Yes, it had to be; I was ... I was in the hospital. My left leg hurt. I could only move my right leg because when I tried to move my left leg, I felt an excruciating pain. I was sore all over. My insides hurt so bad. What was wrong with my insides? I felt like I had been cut open from my breasts to the bottom of my stomach.

I tried to talk, but I couldn't. Why couldn't I talk? I tried but it hurt, and the more I tried to talk, the more it hurt. I felt as if I was in a dream. I was dizzy and confused. I could tell there was something going down my throat; it hurt, and I tried to lift my hands to pull it out. But I couldn't lift them. My left hand hurt tremendously. What was wrong with it? Why did it hurt like this? Why couldn't I move my hands? Were my hands strapped down? Yes, they were. I couldn't get them loose. I tried and tried, but I couldn't. Why were they strapped down? Why? If I could loosen them, I would pull out all these tubes that were down my throat so I could talk.

I later learned that indeed my left leg had been shattered and that four ribs on the left side and three ribs on the right side had been broken. My bowels had been cut almost in half. They had to sew them back together. They also had to remove my spleen. That is why it felt like I had been cut open from my breasts to below my stomach because they had to remove my spleen. My left wrist had been broken. Then everything went blank.

I awoke again. I was trying to figure out where I was. I was not in the hospital as I had been earlier. Where was I? It was dark, completely dark, scary dark. I felt as if I was floating in a three-dimensional world. I began to hear scary, screeching voices crying out at me. The sound began low and grew louder and louder. As the voices grew louder, I began to see these horrible, evil faces. They were far away at first, but as the voices grew, the faces came closer to me.

I was so frightened. There were evil, horrible faces with blood-red eyes and faces with sharp teeth sticking out of their mouths. They were crunching, making loud, awful sounds as if they were going to eat me. They had long arms with sharp claws on the end of each finger. They were unlike any monster I had ever seen. I had seen a lot of scary movies on television in my seventy-five years, but none of them would compare to these horrible, evil faces. This was not a television show. This was real.

These demons made me feel so afraid. That's all I could think of to call them because they were so gruesome looking: demons. I tried and tried to get away from them, but I couldn't. They came closer and closer, and the sound got louder and louder at a higher and higher pitch. They were so close to me now. They were only inches from my face. Their claws were trying to attack me. They kept trying to pull me down into this darkness. I was so terrified. One monster looked like a jack-in-the-box with two heads. It was trying to pull me in. The voices became so loud and at such a high pitch that I couldn't stand them anymore.

I couldn't figure out where I was. *What is this place?* I wondered. Everyone was screaming. It sounded like everyone was being tortured. The screaming kept getting louder and louder, and these demons were flashing their claws in my face. They didn't touch me, but they were so close to my face. It smelled as if everything was burning. It was an awful sulphur smell. I felt as if the heat was going to melt my body. I was trying to get away, but I could not. I could only feel the pain of the heat and the sweat pouring off my body. Everything was burning, and they were trying to pull me in. I was screaming, and tears were rolling down my face. I was holding my hands over my ears, trying to stop the horrible sounds, but they would not stop. I could not stand this anymore. *Please get me out of this place*, I thought.

Then, right when I thought these evil creatures had me, someone warm and peaceful and kind and loving came down and held me in his arms and pulled me away from there. Who was this? Could it be? It couldn't have been anyone else. It had to be Jesus. My Jesus grabbed me and held me in his arms and pulled me out of this terrifying place, and everything was okay again. The same Jesus had put his arm around my two great-granddaughters in the wreck and made them stop screaming. He gave them a peace beyond understanding, and now he was giving me that same peace.

Then it started all over again. I could hear the screams again, but they were far away. Then they started getting louder and louder and closer and closer again. I was crying and screaming for help, but there was none. This kept on until I couldn't stand it anymore. The demons from hell were trying to pull me into hell itself. This place had to be hell. It couldn't be anything else. Jesus was showing me hell. This place was so horrible. I couldn't stand the sound, and the evil demons were right in my face, trying to claw me. Then Jesus came to save me again, and I experienced this warm, loving, kind, and peaceful feeling unlike anything I had felt before. Only Jesus could give you a feeling like this.

It all started over one more time. Three times in all. I went to the gates of hell. Yes, the gates of hell. Yes, I saw this place where the demons were, the place that we call hell. Three times Jesus saved me from this awful place. When Jesus saved me and put his arms around me the third time, I could see clouds and I was going through them. It seemed as if I was floating through the air. Then I saw the most beautiful place I had ever seen in my entire seventy-five years on this earth.

I looked into the clouds and I saw my husband, Pepa; yes, it was him. He was in heaven. He had the biggest smile on his face, and it was shining so brightly. I'm not sure if he could see me or not. He was building something. I couldn't talk to him, but I did see him. I know Jesus let me see him just to let me know he was there. I was not in heaven all the way, but I was at the edge of heaven looking in and I saw him. I saw Pepa, my loving husband, in heaven.

I also could see this lush patch of green, green grass. It was unlike any place I had ever seen. It made me feel so warm and peaceful, so full of *love*. There were beautiful white clouds. This place was so bright. My eyes could barely withstand the brightness. And then I saw her: my Baby Sandra Sue. She was sitting in the middle of this beautiful patch of green, green grass. I could see her through all the brightness. Jesus held me in his arms and took me to heaven. I knew it; I knew this place was heaven.

I had never in all my life felt so much love. Jesus really took me to heaven. I didn't get to go into heaven, but I was right there where I could see inside. My Baby Sandra Sue had two babies with her. I knew at that moment that she had died and gone to heaven, but I felt no sorrow or hurt in my heart.

What I heard next I will never forget as long as I live. My Baby Sandra Sue, in a soft, sweet, angelic voice, said, "Mother, I am okay, so don't be sad for me. I have never felt so much love and peace in all my Life. I am with my baby, Skeet. I have waited so long to be with my baby. Now I am right here with him. I would not go back even if I could. Here in this place no one judges me or gets mad at me. I can be myself. I don't make anyone mad at me anymore. I am happier now than I have ever been. You cannot even understand how much love is in this place."

When my Baby Sandra Sue told me this, I felt so peaceful inside. I knew that she was with the baby she had lost eleven hours after carrying him for nine months. She had waited so long to be with Skeet. But who was this other baby that she held in her arms? I could see her; she had long, curly blond hair. So I asked my Baby Sandra Sue, "Who is this baby you are holding?" What she told me would change my life forever. She said, "Mom, this is my Baby Sandra Sue. After I had my first girl, Christy, I became pregnant again, but after three months I had a miscarriage. I carried this baby inside me for three months. This is that baby I miscarried. This is *my* Baby Sandra Sue."

I thought to myself, *Baby Sandra Sue had her own Baby Sandra Sue.*

Then she said something to me that I hope will change the whole world. She looked right at me with her face shining as bright as ever, and in that angelic voice, Sandra said, "Mother, I want you to tell all the women that you see that if they have had a miscarriage, their baby is here in heaven with Jesus." I looked up and I saw a great host of babies. Yes, a great host of babies in heaven, and they were laughing and smiling. They looked so happy, and their faces were shining so brightly. I could barely look at them they were so bright. The joy and love that I felt at this moment was unlike anything I had ever experienced.

Then my Baby Sandra Sue said, "Mom, tell the women who have had an abortion that this is a sin just like the rest of the sins we commit, and that Jesus will forgive their sins, and that their babies are here too. Yes, those babies are here too." The main thing that my Baby Sandra Sue wanted me to tell the world is this: You, woman or man (because the baby also comes from the man, and he sometimes plays a role in choosing to abort the baby), can see your baby again if you just let Jesus into your heart and believe that he died on the cross to take away your sins. Then you will go to heaven and be with your babies again, just like my Baby Sandra Sue did. She went to heaven and was reunited with Skeet and her unborn Baby Sandra Sue.

Then I was out again.

When I awoke, I thought that this situation had to be a dream; it couldn't be real. But I knew deep down inside that it was real, that a black truck hit us. The roar of that truck, the screeching of metal scraping, the screaming of my great-granddaughters, and the cries of my Baby Sandra Sue all made this horrible feeling swell up in my chest on top of the physical pain I had.

Now all I could think about were Kathy and Miranda. Were they okay? I kept trying to ask everyone where they were. I had all those tubes down my throat and was unable to speak, so I had to motion with one hand and my eyes. I felt so dizzy and confused. *Lord Jesus, please help me*, I prayed. *Tell me that my great-granddaughters are okay*. Then I opened my eyes and saw my son. I held up two fingers, and I heard him say that Kathy and Miranda were upstairs and they were okay. Even though no one told me, I knew my Baby Sandra Sue had died in this accident. I had seen her in heaven.

I had wanted to stay in heaven with my Baby Sandra Sue, but Jesus told me that it was not my time. He wanted me to tell the world what my Baby Sandra Sue had told me about their babies, that they were in heaven waiting for them, even the aborted ones. Jesus also told me that he had things for me to do, so I could not stay. I know for the longest time I was in a three-dimensional place somewhere between heaven and hell. I can tell you this: each one of you will have to make a choice whether or not to accept what

51

Jesus says. You will have to decide to let Jesus into your heart and believe that he died on a cross to pay for your sins. Or you can make the choice to ignore the call of Jesus and not ask him into your heart and not believe what he did for you. You will have to decide if there is more to life after you die and where you will spend the rest of your life after you die. What will you do? What choice will you make? Where will you spend your life after you die?

heaven or hell?

CHAPTER 8

THE MESSAGE

When I woke up again, I was in the hospital. I knew this time it was not a dream. I saw my son standing next to my bed. Lewis was looking at me and holding my hand. I tried to tell him that I had died and gone to heaven. I pointed to the heavens and tried to say I had died, but the words wouldn't come out. Those freaking tubes were in the way, and they kept me from talking. My son didn't understand me. It made me mad. He kept saying, "No, Mema, you didn't die. You are in the hospital. You are alive." My son said, "If you get to go to heaven before I get to go to heaven, I will be so mad." Then he pointed up to heaven.

For the past five years, we had always teased each other about who would get to go to heaven first. I always told him I was older than he was so I should get to go first. My son just didn't understand that I was trying to tell him that I had died and gone to heaven. He thought I was telling him I wanted to go to heaven, but I wasn't. I was trying to tell him I had been there. Then I guess I went out again.

I woke up yet again, and I was still in the hospital. I

looked up, and at the foot of my bed was my grandson, Lewis's other son, Jack. It was his birthday. They had a birthday cake, and they were singing happy birthday to him. It was July 30. I had been in the hospital, in ICU, since July 18, twelve days. This was the first time I really knew what was happening to me. I was still dizzy and confused, but I was starting to understand what was happening.

I noticed our two friends from church standing next to my son. I was surprised to see them. I couldn't talk to them because of the tubes in my throat. I was trying to tell them that I had died and gone to heaven. I could only move my one hand and my lips. At first they couldn't understand what I was trying to say. Then our friend got it; she shouted out, "You died and you went to heaven."

I nodded my head yes, and my eyes lit up. I could feel my face turn red with joy because someone finally had figured out what I was trying to tell them. I was so excited because I had seen heaven and hell and I finally got to tell someone who understood. When something like that happens in your life, you want to tell everyone you see. I wanted to shout it from the mountaintops so everyone could hear me.

I did, I really did. I had died and gone to heaven and saw my husband. Jesus wanted to give me peace about my husband being in heaven because that's what Jesus does: he gives you peace. I know now that my husband went to heaven and is waiting for me; I saw him there. I know he is helping Jesus build me a mansion in heaven. He built highways when he was on this earth. Now he is helping Jesus build me a mansion.

I can't wait to see it and live in it and be reunited with my husband in heaven. This time we will never have to part.

The Bible tells us we will live there for eternity. In John 3:16, the Bible says, "For God so loved the world that he gave his only Son, that whoever believes in him should not perish but have eternal life."

I also saw my Baby Sandra Sue and Skeet and her Baby Sandra Sue. I know the Lord used my daughter to encourage me to tell the whole world that if any woman has a miscarriage or even an abortion, she will be able to see her unborn baby again. The babies are waiting for you to get to heaven. Then you will be joined together with them, just as my Baby Sandra Sue was.

I know that I had been in some type of a dimension between heaven and hell. I know that the demons kept trying to pull me down to hell. (This is what the demons do here on this earth. They try to get you to not believe.) Then Jesus came and pulled me back and showed me heaven. Believe me, you do not want to go to hell. I have truly seen hell. I was at the gates of hell, and I saw it. Please, please listen to me: *Do not say no* to Jesus when he gives you the chance to accept him. This place called hell is not where you want to go, not even for a second. It is horrible. It is such an evil place. It is full of demons, and everything smells like it is burning. It has an awful sulphur odor. I felt so lonesome and all alone, and I did not even go into hell. I only went to the gates of hell, and that was enough for me.

I pray and hope that not one person, no matter how sinful he or she is, will ever go to hell.

Heaven is where you want to go. It is so beautiful and peaceful, and you feel so much love in heaven. You will get to see all the people in your life who went to heaven before you. There will be no sadness, no tears, and no pain ever, and I mean ever. You will not even be able to sin, and no one else will be able to sin either. There will be no more curse from Adam and Eve's sin. You will live forever with Jesus.

I promise you that you do not want to go to hell. You want to go to heaven. So if you have not asked Jesus into your heart, please talk to him right now. Ask him to enter your heart and forgive you for all of your sins. Tell him you believe that he died on the cross to pay for your sins and that he will take away your sins. Tell Jesus you believe that he rose from the grave and went to heaven so you can be with him when you die.

It is not just saying a prayer; you also have to believe that he truly takes away your sins.

You see, the thing that makes heaven so good is that there are no sins there. You cannot sin in heaven. The Bible says in Romans 3:23, "For all have sinned and fall short of the glory of God." Everyone on this earth sins, and if this is true, how do you get to heaven? You have to believe that Jesus died on the cross to pay for your sins and that he takes away your sins, and if you do, you no longer will have your sins. It is not anything you do on your own. You can't earn it or buy it; it is a free gift from God. All you have to do is believe this is true and you will be able to get to heaven. Jesus does the rest.

The Bible says in Romans 6:23, "For the wages of sin is death, but the free gift of God is eternal life in Christ Jesus our Lord." Just welcome him into your heart. Romans 10:9–10 says, "If you confess with your mouth that Jesus is Lord and believe in your heart that God raised him from the dead, you will be saved. For with the heart one believes and is justified, and with the mouth one confesses and is saved."

If after reading this you let Jesus into your heart and believe, then you will need to find a good church and get involved so you can learn as much as you can about Jesus and how to get to know him better. God loves you so much that he gave his one and only son so you can go to heaven and spend eternity with him.

My Baby Sandra Sue is gone from this world forever. All that remains are the precious memories in my heart and knowing that I will someday rejoice with her in paradise for eternity. You can do the same. It's your choice. Jesus loves you so much, and this is

the message.

THE END

Printed in the United States
By Bookmasters